Kentucky

BY ANN HEINRICHS

Content Adviser: Russell Harris, Associate Editor, Kentucky Historical Society, Frankfort, Kentucky

Reading Adviser: Dr. Linda D. Labbo, Department of Reading Education, College of Education, The University of Georgia

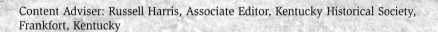
COMPASS POINT BOOKS ✦ MINNEAPOLIS, MINNESOTA

Compass Point Books
3109 West 50th Street, #115
Minneapolis, MN 55410

Visit Compass Point Books on the Internet at *www.compasspointbooks.com*
or e-mail your request to *custserv@compasspointbooks.com*

On the cover: Federal Hall in Bardstown, which is said to be the inspiration for Stephen Foster's song, "My Old Kentucky Home"

Photographs ©: Gary W. Carter/Corbis, cover, 1; Adam Jones, 3, 7, 9, 10, 11, 19, 22, 25, 30, 34, 35, 42, 43 (top), 45, 48 (top); Kent & Donna Dannen, 4, 6, 27, 36, 38, 39, 47; Corbis, 12; Ann Ronan Picture Library, 13, 16, 46; Bettmann/Corbis, 14; Topham Picturepoint, 15, 28, 41; Raymond Gehman/ Corbis, 17, 37; W.L. McCoy, 18, 29; Kevin R. Morris/Corbis, 21, 24, 31; Kevin Fleming/Corbis, 23; Owen Franken/Corbis, 26; Gamma/Mark Cowan/UPI, 32; Topham/Image Works, 40; Robesus, Inc, 43 (state flag); One Mile Up, Inc., 43 (state seal); Gary W. Carter/Visuals Unlimited, 44 (top); DigitalVision, 44 (middle); Artville, 44 (bottom).

Editors: E. Russell Primm, Emily J. Dolbear, and Catherine Neitge
Photo Researchers: Svetlana Zhurkina and Image Select International
Photo Selector: Linda S. Koutris
Designer/Page production: The Design Lab/Jaime Martens
Cartographer: XNR Productions, Inc.

Library of Congress Cataloging-in-Publication Data
Heinrichs, Ann.
  Kentucky / by Ann Heinrichs.
      v. cm.— (This land is your land)
Includes bibliographical references and index.
Contents: Welcome to Kentucky!—Mountains, valleys, and plains—A trip through time—Government by the people—Kentuckians at work—Getting to know Kentuckians—Let's explore Kentucky!— Important dates.
  ISBN 0-7565-0322-1 (hardcover)
1. Kentucky—Juvenile literature. [1. Kentucky.] I. Title.
  F451.3 .H45 2003
  976.9—dc21   2002010056

Table of Contents

NOTE: In this book, words that are defined in the glossary are in **bold** the first time they appear in the text.

▲ Kentucky is known around the world for its wonderful horses.

Daniel Boone explored Kentucky in the 1700s. One day, he stood high atop a mountain. He looked in one direction and saw fertile plains. He looked in another direction and saw forest-covered mountains. They were so high that their tops reached the clouds.

Much of Kentucky still looks the way Boone saw it. Its high mountains touch the sky. Wild animals live in its deep forests. Green, grassy fields stretch as far as the eye can see.

Brave **pioneers** built homes in Kentucky's wild forests. Kentuckians today still have the spirit of those pioneers. They know they can do any hard job.

Kentuckians make cars, trucks, and many other products today. Kentucky's racehorses are famous around the world. The mountains and forests, however, still welcome new explorers. Now you can explore Kentucky, too!

▲ Rich farmland lies along the Ohio River in Kentucky.

Most of Kentucky's borders are bumpy and crooked. They are formed by mountains and rivers. The Appalachian Mountains rise up on the east. On the west is the great Mississippi River. The Ohio River forms Kentucky's northern border and flows into the Mississippi.

Kentucky's southern border is almost a straight line. Tennessee is Kentucky's neighbor to the south. Virginia and West Virginia lie to the east. Missouri is across the Mississippi River to the west. Ohio, Indiana, and Illinois are north of Kentucky.

Eastern Kentucky has many mountains and valleys. In the southeast are Cumberland Mountain and Pine Mountain. These formations are part of the Appalachian Mountains. Some people call this area the Eastern Coalfield because rich supplies of coal lie underground.

▲ **Pine Mountain in southeastern Kentucky**

Far-western Kentucky is a low-lying plain. The large center part of Kentucky is a plateau, an area of high, flat land. This region is higher than the western plains but lower than the eastern mountains.

North-central Kentucky is called the Bluegrass Region. It's named for the grass on its rolling plains. The grass itself is not blue, but its dusty flowers are. When they bloom, the ground takes on a faint blue color. Many horse farms are in this region. So are Lexington and Louisville, Kentucky's largest cities.

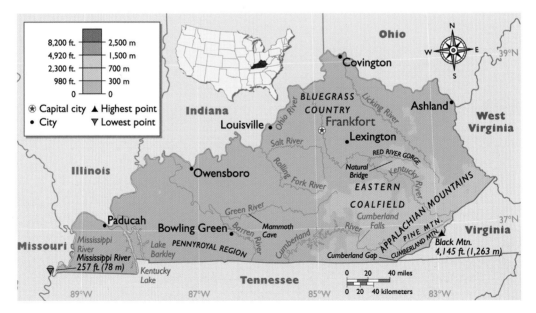

▲ **A topographic map of Kentucky**

▲ The Bluegrass hills at sunrise

▲ **Formations in the Drapery Room at Mammoth Cave National Park**

Part of south-central Kentucky is called the Pennyroyal Region. It's named for the pennyroyal, a little mint plant. The many underground caves in this region include Mammoth Cave. It's the world's longest chain of caves.

Forests cover almost half of Kentucky's land. Wolves and moose once lived there. Sadly, hunting has killed them all. Deer, foxes, rabbits, and raccoons still roam the forests, though. Black bears and elk were once wiped out by hunting. They have now been reintroduced to Kentucky's mountains and forests.

Kentucky has cool winters and warm summers. Spring is a rainy season there. The southern border gets the heaviest rainfall. The southeastern mountains get the most snow, but northern Kentucky has the coldest winter weather.

▲ Louisville gets snowy winters.

▲ **Many Native Americans, including
the Shawnee, hunted in Kentucky.**

People have lived in Kentucky for thousands of years. Ancient people hunted animals and grew crops. They buried their dead in mounds—piles of earth and stones. Later, many Native American groups hunted in Kentucky. They were the Shawnee, the Chickasaw, and the Cherokee peoples.

By the 1700s, people from Europe were moving in. England organized thirteen **colonies** along the Atlantic Ocean. Kentucky was part of the Virginia colony. At first, settlers could not easily reach

Kentucky. Mountains and forests stood in their way. In 1750, however, Thomas Walker discovered the Cumberland Gap—a break in Kentucky's eastern mountains.

▲ Settlers passed through the Cumberland Gap in covered wagons.

Daniel Boone arrived in 1767. Later he led many pioneers into bluegrass country. James Harrod set up Harrodsburg in 1774. This was Kentucky's first town, and it still exists. Daniel Boone founded Boonesborough in 1775.

Native Americans watched the pioneers take over their land. Also in 1775, a company owned by white settlers purchased a huge piece of land from the Indians. Most of that land is now part of Kentucky. One of the chiefs present at the signing of the treaty said of the land, "There is a dark cloud over that Country." Another chief told Daniel Boone, "Brother, we have given you a fine land, but I believe you will have much trouble settling it." Many battles were fought as the white settlers took over more and more of the Native Americans' ancient homelands.

▲ **Daniel Boone**

▲ Colonists fought against the British during the Revolutionary War.

The colonists began to wish for their freedom from Great Britain. They fought the Revolutionary War (1775–1783). At last, the colonists won! Their new country was now called the United States. Kentucky became the fifteenth state in 1792.

Soon, thousands of settlers poured into Kentucky. They raised cattle, corn, and tobacco.

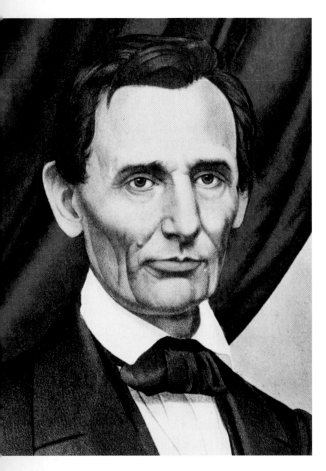

▲ **President Lincoln came from a pioneer family.**

The Lincolns were one pioneer family. Their son, Abraham, became the sixteenth U.S. president in 1861.

Meanwhile, slavery was tearing America apart. Southern states wanted slavery, but Northern states were against it. Eleven of these Southern states with-drew from the Union and formed the Confederate States of America. Their actions led to the Civil War (1861–1865).

Some Kentuckians had slaves. At first, Kentucky want-ed to be **neutral,** but most Kentuckians chose to remain in the Union. There were Kentuckians fighting on both sides, however. President Lincoln guided the United States through the war and preserved the Union.

After the war, coal mining became a big **industry** in Kentucky. Large companies controlled Kentucky's tobacco industry, but tobacco farmers fought them. Eventually, tobacco farmers shared control with government and industry. Kentucky also became famous for breeding horses.

▲ **A tobacco barn east of Berea**

In the 1930s, the United States faced hard times. Like workers in other states, many Kentuckians lost their jobs. Things began to get better during World War II (1939–1945). Kentucky's farms, factories, and mines produced war supplies.

Kentucky grew quickly after the war. Coal mining brought in even more money. By the 1980s, many new factories made cars and trucks. More tourists are discovering Kentucky every day now. They enjoy its many historic places and natural scenic areas.

▲ **Smokestacks from a Kentucky power plant**

Government by the People

▲ Kentucky's state capitol is in Frankfort.

Kentucky's full name is the Commonwealth of Kentucky.
That name comes from Kentucky's early history. A commonwealth is a government that agrees to work for the good of all
the people.

The United States's national government has three branches.
They are the legislative, executive, and judicial branches. The
ruling power is split three ways so that no branch can get too
powerful. Kentucky's state government is set up in the same way.

Kentucky's legislative branch makes the state laws. It also decides how the state will spend its money. Voters choose their lawmakers. Those lawmakers serve in Kentucky's general assembly. It has two houses, or parts. One house is the thirty-eight-member senate. The other house is the one hundred-member house of representatives.

The executive branch makes sure the state's laws are obeyed. Kentucky's governor is the head of the executive branch. Kentuckians vote to choose a governor every four years. The governor has a cabinet, or group of assistants. They carry out many executive jobs.

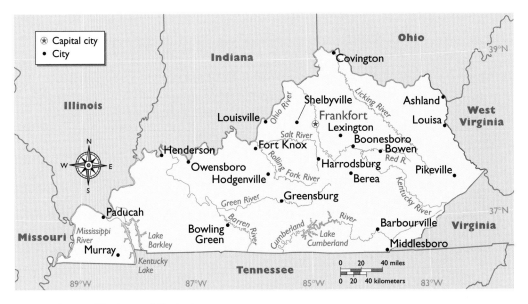

▲ **A geopolitical map of Kentucky**

▲ Beautiful rowhouses line this street in Mason County.

Kentucky's judges and courts make up the judicial branch. The judges know a lot about Kentucky's laws. They decide whether a person or group has broken the law. Kentucky's highest court is the Kentucky Supreme Court.

Kentucky is divided into 120 counties. Most counties are governed by a fiscal court. Kentucky's cities and towns elect a mayor or city manager. Cities and towns elect lawmakers, too. They serve on a city council.

▲ **Fort Knox**

Imagine a gold bar the size of an ordinary building brick. It weighs about 27½ pounds (12 kilograms), and it's worth $17,000. Now hold that thought because it's the closest you will ever get to that gold brick. That brick—and $6 billion worth of others like it—are kept in a building at Fort Knox, near Louisville. No visitors are allowed. The U.S. government stores its gold there. This gold helps to maintain the value of American money.

Kentuckians make money in many ways. One way is by selling products such as coal. Kentucky is one of the top coal-mining states. Kentucky's factories are busy, too. Their major products are trucks and cars. Kentucky also makes cleaning products, medicines, and machines.

▲ Louisville slugger baseball bats are among Kentucky's most famous products.

▲ A horse, which is about to have a foal, grazes in Fayette County. Kentucky is a famous horse-breeding center.

White fences run for miles in the Bluegrass Region. They mark the borders of horse farms. Kentucky is called the "horse capital of the world." The horses nibble on the tasty bluegrass. It is known to be a healthful food for them. Some grow up to be the world's fastest racehorses.

Tobacco is Kentucky's most important crop. Kentucky leads all states in growing a kind of tobacco called burley. Kentucky farmers also raise corn, cattle, hogs, and chickens. Some of the chickens end up as Kentucky Fried Chicken.

▲ Hay bales on a farm near Greenup

▲ **Harland Sanders, founder of the Kentucky Fried Chicken chain of restaurants**

Have you ever heard of Colonel Harland Sanders? His picture is on all Kentucky Fried Chicken restaurants. In the picture, he wears a white suit and has a fluffy little beard. Sanders began his famous restaurant chain with a secret chicken recipe. He started serving chicken from his Kentucky gas station. He died in 1980 at the age of ninety.

Kentuckians have several products to sell. However, most Kentucky workers sell services. They may work in schools, hospitals, banks, or stores. Some work on the computers that make factories run. Some service workers guard the gold at Fort Knox. Some train horses. They all help Kentucky make money and run smoothly.

▲ A trainer works with a Thoroughbred horse at a special training facility.

Pioneers in Kentucky had to be strong people. They built their own homes, found their food, and tried to keep their children safe. Families stuck together and helped each other. Today, almost half of Kentuckians still live in **rural** areas.

▲ **A rural Kentuckian works on a farm in Appalachia.**

▲ **Modern musicians play Kentucky folk music.**

Most early settlers came to Kentucky from eastern states. They had roots in England, Scotland, and Ireland. Many African-Americans lived in Kentucky in the early 1800s. Today only about one of every fourteen Kentuckians is African-American.

In 2000, more than 4 million people lived in Kentucky. At census time, Lexington was the largest city. In 2003, however, Louisville will become a metropolitan government and will be Kentucky's largest city by far.

Much of America's **folk** music came from Kentucky. Mountain people sang English, Scottish, and Irish songs. Bluegrass music also grew out of Kentucky's **traditions.** Many Kentucky towns have bluegrass music festivals.

▲ A man demonstrates basket weaving in Louisville.

Kentuckians are good at folk **crafts,** too. They make hand-made quilts, baskets, furniture, and dolls. Many of them show off their work in Berea. This town holds an arts and crafts fair every May.

"'Tis a gift to be simple, 'Tis a gift to be free." This is how the song "Simple Gifts" starts. It is one of the best-known songs of the Shaker religious group. Shakers settled in Kentucky in the 1800s. They made everything they needed by hand. Today, South Union Shaker Village and Shaker Village of Pleasant Hill carry on their customs. Many festivals and craft shows are held at the two places.

▲ **Shaker Village of Pleasant Hill carries on Shaker customs.**

The Kentucky Derby horse race is a huge event. It is held each year in Louisville on the first Saturday in May. Kentuckians hold many other exciting horse races and horse shows.

Thousands of people attend the Daniel Boone Festival in Barbourville every October. People celebrate with pioneer costumes, dancing, and food. It's a great way to enjoy Kentucky's history today.

▲ **Horses race around the first turn in the Kentucky Derby in Louisville.**

Let's Explore Kentucky!

If you visit Kentucky, be sure to visit Mammoth Cave. With more than 335 miles (539 km) of mapped passages, it is the longest cave in the world. It can be quite an exciting place to explore! You'll wander down spooky paths. All of a sudden, you'll enter giant rooms. Long, pointy rocks hang from the ceiling. Others rise up from the floor. In one room, Mammoth Dome towers high over-head. There is even an underground waterway called the Green River.

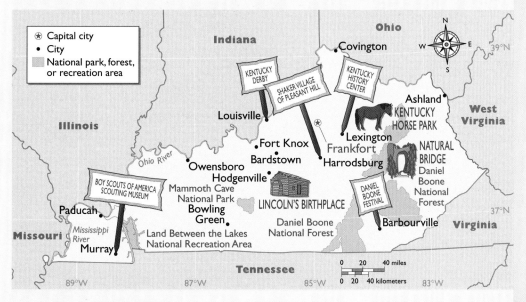

▲ **Places to visit in Kentucky**

▲ **Scenic Eagle Falls**

You've seen a rainbow. But have you ever seen a moon-bow? You'll see one at Cumberland Falls. This waterfall sends up a mist, or tiny drops of water. If you look through that mist when the moon is full, you will see a many-colored moonbow!

Cumberland Falls is in Daniel Boone National Forest. So is Red River Gorge. The Red River cut this deep valley through rock, creating many colors and strange shapes. Nearby is Natural Bridge. It developed naturally from solid rock.

▲ **Natural Bridge in Daniel Boone National Forest**

Do you like horses? You'll want to check out the Kentucky Horse Park in Lexington. You'll watch a parade of more than forty breeds of horses. Want to see even more horses? There are horse farms all around Lexington, and many of them welcome visitors.

▲ **A Kentuckian participating in the Parade of Breeds in Lexington**

▲ **Bison graze in the Land Between the Lakes National Recreation Area.**

Land Between the Lakes is in western Kentucky. It's home to a herd of bison, or buffalo. They are protected there so they can live safely. Another area has a farm like those of the 1800s. Visitors also enjoy a nature center and **planetarium.**

In Frankfort, you can visit the state capitol and watch the lawmakers at work. Many statues of famous Kentuckians stand in the capitol. At the nearby Kentucky History Center, you'll see Daniel Boone's hand-written notes. You'll also follow the history of civil rights in Kentucky.

▲ A woman shows how to spin yarn as Shakers did in the 1800s.

Have you ever wondered how to make candles? Or were you ever curious how to use a spinning wheel or make a broom? You can learn these skills at Shaker Village of Pleasant Hill. Workers at the village will show you how the Shakers lived.

Abraham Lincoln was born near Hodgenville. When he was two years old, the family moved to a farm on nearby Knob Creek. The little log cabin that stands there today is just like Lincoln's boyhood home. You'll see what a tiny place he lived in!

▲ **This log cabin is just like the one Abraham Lincoln lived in from age two to seven.**

▲ Stephen Foster

"My Old Kentucky Home" is Kentucky's state song. Stephen Foster wrote it. According to one legend, Foster once visited relatives who lived in Bardstown. He loved their home so much, he wrote the song. Actually, the song was probably inspired by a fictional slave in Harriet Beecher Stowe's book *Uncle Tom's Cabin* (1852). Foster named the first version of his song "Poor Uncle Tom, Good Night."

The chorus assured Uncle Tom that he was "bound for a better land." Anyone who's been in Kentucky will surely agree that it is a land filled with a rich history and an exciting future.

Important Dates

1750   Thomas Walker explores Kentucky.

1767   Daniel Boone travels through Kentucky.

1774   Harrodsburg is Kentucky's first European settlement.

1792   Kentucky becomes the fifteenth state on June 1.

1861   Kentucky wants to be neutral in the Civil War but remains in the Union.

1904–1909   Kentucky tobacco farmers fight the Black Patch War.

1937   The United States begins keeping gold at Fort Knox.

1955   Eighteen-year-old Kentuckians can vote.

1966   Kentucky passes a civil rights law.

1978   Kentucky Horse Park opens near Lexington.

1983   Martha Layne Collins becomes Kentucky's first female governor.

1990   Kentucky makes changes in its public school system to improve education.

1999   Nicki Patton and Ellen Williams are elected chairpersons of Kentucky's Democratic and Republican parties. This is the first time in the state's history that both parties are led by women.

Glossary

colonies—territories that belong to the country that settles them

crafts—items made by hand

folk—ordinary people

industry—a business or trade

neutral—not taking any side in an argument

pioneers— people who explore or settle in a new land

planetarium—a building where people study stars and planets

rural—of the countryside; away from cities and towns

traditions—customs that are common among a family or group

Did You Know?

★ The Kentucky Derby is the oldest continuously run horse race in the United States. It's also the oldest continuously held sporting event of any kind in all of North America. It's one of the three races that make up the Triple Crown of U.S. horse racing. The other two are the Preakness in Maryland and the Belmont Stakes in New York. The two-week-long Kentucky Derby Festival opens with the world's largest fireworks display.

★ The first cheeseburger was served in 1934 at Kaelin's restaurant in Louisville.

★ In 1980, Joe Bowen set the world record for walking on stilts. He traveled 3,008 miles (4,841 km) from Bowen, Kentucky, to Los Angeles, California.

★ Smiley Pete, the "town dog" of Lexington, died in 1957. Now he's honored with a brass plate in the sidewalk in downtown Lexington.

★ The Boy Scouts of America Scouting Museum is in Murray.

State capital: Frankfort

State motto: United We Stand, Divided We Fall

State nickname: Bluegrass State

Statehood: June 1, 1792; fifteenth state

Area: 40,411 square miles (104,665 sq km); **rank:** thirty-seventh

Highest point: Black Mountain, 4,145 feet (1,263 m) above sea level

Lowest point: Along the Mississippi River in Fulton County, 257 feet (78 m) above sea level

Highest recorded temperature: 114°F (46°C) at Greensburg on July 28, 1930

Lowest recorded temperature: −37°F (−38°C) at Shelbyville on January 19, 1994

Average January temperature: 34°F (1°C)

Average July temperature: 77°F (25°C)

Population in 2000: 4,041,769; **rank:** twenty-fifth

Largest cities in 2000: Lexington (260,512), Louisville (256,231), Owensboro (54,067), Bowling Green (49,296)

Factory products: Cars and trucks, chemicals, tobacco products

Farm products: Tobacco, beef cattle, horses

Mining products: Coal

State flag: Kentucky's state flag shows the state seal. The seal appears against a blue field.

State seal: The state seal shows two men shaking hands. One wears frontier clothes. The other wears a suit. Around them is the state motto: "United We Stand, Divided We Fall." Some say the men are a frontiersman and a government leader. Others say they are a Kentuckian and his Virginia neighbor. The handshake shows that they respect each other. At the top are the words "Commonwealth of Kentucky"—Kentucky's official name. At the bottom are goldenrod branches. Goldenrod is the state flower.

State abbreviations: Ky. or Ken. (traditional); KY (postal)

State Symbols

State bird: Kentucky cardinal

State flower: Goldenrod

State tree: Tulip poplar

State wild animal: Gray squirrel

State fish: Kentucky bass

State horse: Thoroughbred

State butterfly: Viceroy butterfly

State gemstone: Freshwater pearl

State fossil: *Brachiopod*

State bluegrass song: "Blue Moon of Kentucky"

State commemorative quarter: Released on October 15, 2001

Making Fried Green Tomatoes

Fried green tomatoes are a favorite Kentucky treat.

Makes four servings.

INGREDIENTS:

4 large green tomatoes

2 cups cornmeal

1/2 teaspoon salt

2 eggs

1/4 cup vegetable oil

DIRECTIONS:

Make sure an adult helps with the cutting and cooking. Slice the tomatoes into 1/4-inch slices. Mix the cornmeal and salt in a bowl. Beat the eggs. Dip the tomato slices in the beaten eggs. Then dip the tomato slices in the cornmeal until they're coated. Heat the vegetable oil in a frying pan. Use low to medium heat. (Lower heat makes them crispy!) Fry the coated tomato slices until they're golden brown. Remove tomato slices and place them on a paper towel to soak up the extra oil. Note: Some people like to melt cheese on top before eating.

"My Old Kentucky Home"

Words and music by Stephen Collins Foster

The sun shines bright on my old Kentucky home,
'Tis summer, the people are gay;
The corn top's ripe and the meadow's in the bloom,
While the birds make music all the day.

The young folks roll on the little cabin floor,
All merry, all happy and bright;
By'n by hard times comes a-knockin' at the door,
Then my old Kentucky home, good-night!

Weep no more, my lady!
Oh weep no more today.
We will sing one song for my old Kentucky home,
For my old Kentucky home, far away.

Muhammad Ali (1942–) is a world-champion boxer. He was born Cassius Clay in Louisville.

Louis Brandeis (1856–1941) was a U.S. Supreme Court justice (1916–1939). Brandeis was born in Louisville. He was an important supporter of conservation.

Cassius Marcellus Clay (1810–1903) worked to free slaves and end slavery. Clay was born in Madison County. He published the abolitionist paper *The True American* in Lexington.

Henry Clay (1777–1852) was a congressman, U.S. senator, and served as secretary of state. He is best known for achieving the Missouri Compromise of 1820 and the Compromise of 1850. He was born in Virginia and moved to Lexington in 1797.

Jefferson Davis (1808–1889) was president of the Confederate States of America during the Civil War. He was born in Christian (now Todd) County.

John Marshall Harlan (1833–1911) was a U.S. Supreme Court justice (1877–1911). Harlan was born in Boyle County.

Abraham Lincoln (1809–1865) was the sixteenth U.S. president (1861–1865). Lincoln (pictured above left) was born in Hardin County. He led the United States during the Civil War and was shot and killed by John Wilkes Booth in 1865.

Brian Littrell (1975–) is a member of the pop group the Backstreet Boys. Littrell was born in Lexington and is Kevin Richardson's cousin.

Kevin Richardson (1971–) is a member of the pop group the Backstreet Boys. Richardson was born in Lexington and is Brian Littrell's cousin.

Adlai Stevenson (1835–1914) was the U.S. vice president under Grover Cleveland (1893–1897). He was born in Christian (now Todd) County. He was the grandfather of Adlai E. Stevenson II, who was the Democratic nominee for president in 1952 and 1956.

Jesse Stuart (1906–1984) was born in Riverton and wrote stories about life in Kentucky.

Zachary Taylor (1784–1850) was the twelfth U.S. president (1849–1850). He was born in Virginia and grew up near Louisville.

Frederick Vinson (1890–1953) was the chief justice of the U.S. Supreme Court (1946–1953). Vinson was born in Louisa. He was also a member of the U.S. House of Representatives (1923–1929, 1931–1938) and secretary of the treasury (1945).

Want to Know More?

At the Library

Brown, Dottie. *Kentucky.* Minneapolis: Lerner Publications, 1992.

Streissguth, Thomas, and Loren Chantland. *Daniel Boone.* Minneapolis: Carolrhoda Books, 2001.

Stuart, Jesse. *Tales from the Plum Grove Hills.* Ashland, Ky.: Jesse Stuart Foundation, 1998.

Wellsbacher, Anne. *Kentucky.* Edina, Minn.: Abdo & Daughters, 1998.

Williams, Suzanne M. *Kentucky.* Danbury, Conn.: Children's Press, 2001.

Witte-Blank, Grace, and Suzanne Witte-Barrett (illustrator). *Jeannie and Sue Visit a Kentucky Farm.* Venice, Fla.: Feather Fables, 1994.

On the Web

Kentucky GA Website for Kids
http://www.lrc.state.ky.us/kidspage/kidindex.htm
To learn more about Kentucky and its history

KYDirect: The Commonwealth of Kentucky Home Page
http://www.kydirect.net
To visit the state web site, with information on Kentucky's history, government, economy, and land

Through the Mail

Kentucky Department of Travel
P.O. Box 2011
Frankfort, KY 40602
For information on travel and interesting sights in Kentucky

Kentucky Historical Society
100 West Broadway
Frankfort, KY 40601
502/564-1792
For information about Kentucky's history

Kentucky Secretary of State
700 Capital Avenue, Suite 152
State Capitol
Frankfort, KY 40601
For information on Kentucky's state government

On the Road

Kentucky History Center
100 West Broadway
Frankfort, KY 40601
502/564-1792
To learn more about the history of Kentucky

Kentucky State Capitol
700 Capitol Avenue
Frankfort, KY 40601
502/564-3449
To visit Kentucky's capitol

Index

About the Author

Ann Heinrichs grew up in Fort Smith, Arkansas, and lives in Chicago. She is the author of more than eighty books for children and young adults on Asian, African, and U.S. history and culture. Ann has also written numerous newspaper, magazine, and encyclopedia articles. She is an award-winning martial artist, specializing in t'ai chi empty-hand and sword forms.

Ann has traveled widely throughout the United States, Africa, Asia, and the Middle East. In exploring each state for this series, she rediscovered the people, history, and resources that make this a great land, as well as the concerns we share with people around the world.